CHARLIE'S TIME TO SHINE

BY STANLEY GETER, JR

ILLUSTRATED BY SANGHAMITRA DASGUPTA

ACUTE BY DESIGN
the little book company that could

ACUTEBYDESIGN PUBLISHING

TEXT COPYRIGHT © 2022 BY STANLEY GETER, JR

ILLUSTRATIONS COPYRIGHT © 2022 BBY SANGHAMITRA DASGUPTA

ALL RIGHTS RESERVED

FIRST EDITION 2022

ACUTEBYDESIGN.COM

ISBN: 978-1-943515-53-0

LIBRARY OF CONGRESS CATALOGING

2022936068

Dedication

To mom and pops (Pauline and Stanley Geter Sr.) for helping your little boy learn at a young age that I can do anything I set my mind to and that hard work, self-belief and determination can overcome anything life sends my way.

To my loving wife (Melissa), I couldn't have done any of this without you beautiful. You listen to all of my off-the-wall story ideas and always offer unwavering support. You truly believe in me, you cheer me on, you make it all possible and this book would have never seen the light of day without your constant encouragement. I'm lucky to have you by my side and don't take a moment of it for granted.
Thank you for all that you do!

Thank you to my siblings (Paul, Michelle, Crystal, Melanie and Erin), family members and the many friends who lift me up when things get tough and support me on all of my adventures.

Last but not least, to every child, teen or adult who has ever been harrassed, bullied or teased for one of your features, this book is dedicated to you.

This book is the first in a series that explores the image issues that many of us have faced at some point in life. I hope you enjoy Charlie's adventure and come along for the journey of the Schoolhouse Super Squad (Charlie, Larry, Patty, Finneas, and Winnie) as they navigate through the ups and downs of turning perceived weaknesses
into their greatest strengths!

With sincerest gratitude,
Stan Geter Jr.

THAT DREARY NIGHT AS HIS MOTHER PASSED BY THE OLD BEDROOM **DOOR**,
SHE HEARD HIS CRIES OVER HER FOOTSTEPS TAPPING ON THE HARD WOODEN **FLOOR**.

HIS DAY AT SCHOOL WAS A NIGHTMARE AND ONE HE WISHED SOON TO **FORGET**,
BECAUSE THE OTHER KIDS TEASED HIM MERCILESSLY AND SIMPLY WOULD NOT **RELENT**.

"CHARLIE, WHAT'S WRONG BABY, HOW CAN MOMMA HELP, DO YOU WANT TO **TALK**?"
"NO MOM, YOU DON'T UNDERSTAND, YOU DON'T HAVE TEETH
THAT LOOK LIKE BROKEN PIECES OF **CHALK**."

THIS WAS A SLIGHT EXAGGERATION AND OF COURSE,
TEETH MADE OF CHALK WOULD BE HARD TO **BELIEVE**.
THE FAR-FETCHED COMPARISON WAS MERELY AN ANGRY
ATTEMPT TO GET HIS MOTHER TO **LEAVE**.

"WE'RE SEEING A SPECIAL DENTIST IN THE MORNING," SHE SAID
HIS SAD EYES GLUED TO THE **FLOOR**.
HIS SILENCE MADE IT QUITE CLEAR THIS WASN'T A DISCUSSION
SHE SHOULD PURSUE **ANYMORE**.

ONCE HER FOOTSTEPS BECAME FAINT AND HE HEARD HER DOOR CLOSE
CHARLIE SPRANG STRAIGHT FROM HIS **BED**,
FLINGING AWAY THE TEAR DRENCHED BED SHEETS
THAT WERE DRAPED CLUMSILY OVER HIS **HEAD**.

SHUFFLING OVER TO THE MIRROR HE GAVE HIMSELF A LONG, INDIFFERENT **STARE**,
PULLING AWAY FROM HIS EYES HIS RUFFLED, CURLY, DISHEVELED BLACK **HAIR**.

FIRST WAS A FROWN BUT EVENTUALLY THROUGH PURSED LIPS
CAME THE HINT OF A **SMILE**,
THAT REVEALED ROWS UPON ROWS OF CROOKED TEETH
THAT WENT ON FOR WHAT SEEMED LIKE A **MILE**.

HE CURSED THIS "DEFECT" AND PRAYED TO THE LORD ABOVE FOR A **CHANGE**,
BUT EVERY MORNING HE AWOKE TO FIND HIS UNSIGHTLY CHOMPERS
REMAINED EXACTLY THE **SAME**.

WHY HIM, HE QUESTIONED? WHAT DID HE DO TO DESERVE THIS HIDEOUS **FATE**?
HE DID HIS HOMEWORK, HIS CHORES, AVOIDED CANDY AND RARELY ATE ANY **CAKE**.

TIRELESS FLOSSING AND COUNTLESS HOURS SPENT
DILIGENTLY BRUSHING HIS PEARLY **WHITES**,
DIDN'T STOP THEM FROM SPREADING IN
ALL ANGLES LIKE FRIGHTENED BIRDS TAKING **FLIGHT**.

THE TAUNTS, NAME CALLING, AND BULLYING - THE JEERS FROM HIS **PEERS**,
OFTEN LEFT CHARLIE DRENCHED IN MASSIVE PUDDLES OF WARM, SALTY **TEARS**.

"JAWS, CHOMPERS, SNAGGLETOOTH AND PIRANHA BOY,"
WERE ON THE SHORT LIST OF EVIL **NAMES**,
THAT HIS CRUEL CLASSMATES CALLED HIM WHEN THEY PLAYED THEIR
"LET'S MAKE CHARLIE CRY" **GAMES**.

HE CLOSED HIS MOUTH AND GLANCED OVER ANXIOUSLY AT THE NOISY
TICK-TOCKING **CLOCK**,
KNOWING THAT COME MORNING HE'D BE SITTING IN FRONT OF THE
TOOTH STRAIGHTENING **DOC**.

FEAR OVERWHELMED HIM, CONSUMED HIM, FILLED HIM WITH **DREAD**,
AND, TIRED OF STARING AT HIS CURSE IN THE MIRROR,
HE HOPPED BACK INTO THE **BED**.

OFF TO DREAMLAND HE WENT WHERE HIS TEETH WERE PERFECT, PRETTY, AND **STRAIGHT**,
SO MUCH SO HE RECEIVED THE AWARD FOR BEST SMILE FROM ALL OF HIS TEACHERS AND **CLASSMATES**.

IF ONLY THERE WERE A WAY TO MAKE HIS FANTASTICAL DREAMS COME **TRUE**, HIS LIFE WOULD CHANGE DRASTICALLY AND GREY SKIES COULD SWAP FOR SHADES OF **BLUE**.

THE ALARM CLOCK SCREECHED, A HORRIBLE SOUND,
AND PULLED HIM FROM PEACEFUL **SLUMBER**,
OFF TO THE BATHROOM LIKE A CRANKY OGRE CHARLIE BEGAN
TO SLUGGISHLY **LUMBER**.

THROUGH HIS DAILY HYGIENE ROUTINE HE HURRIEDLY **BUSTLED**,
MUMBLING UNDER HIS BREATH WITH WORDS THAT WERE GARBLED AND **JUMBLED**

"I'LL BE WAITING IN THE CAR," HIS MOTHER SHOUTED FROM DOWNSTAIRS,
CAUSING HIM TO **HURRY,**
CHARLIE QUICKENED HIS PACE EVEN FURTHER INTO ONE OF A
FAST FRANTIC **SCURRY.**

HE THREW ON A T-SHIRT, SWEAT PANTS AND FOOTWEAR **APPAREL,**
CLEAN LAUNDRY WAS SCARCE AND HE HAD TO DIG FROM
THE BOTTOM OF THE **BARREL.**

A QUICK GLANCE IN THE MIRROR, AN APPROVING NOD AND A **SHUFFLE**
OUT TO MEET HIS MOTHER IN THE CAR DOUBLE-TIME LEST HE CAUSE A **KERFUFFLE.**

THE CAR RIDE TO THE ORTHODONTIST WAS QUIET
AND NOT MANY WORDS WERE **SPOKEN,**
THE BOND BETWEEN THE BOY AND HIS REGULAR DENTIST
WAS STRONG AND COULD NOT BE **BROKEN.,**

THIS NEW GUY EVEN HAD A FUNNY NAME, DOCTOR EDWARD **NAMMELL**,
HIS NAME RHYMED WITH WORDS LIKE SHAMBLE, GAMBLE
AND CHARLIE'S FAVORITE, THE HUMPED-BACK **CAMEL**.

AS THEY PULLED UP TO THE OFFICE HE STARED IN WONDER AND **AWE**,
THE UNBELIEVABLE SCENERY CAUSED AN IMMEDIATE DROP OF HIS **JAW**.

SHRUBS WERE EXPERTLY CARVED INTO TOOTHBRUSHES AND TEETH,
AND EVEN FLOSS **PICKS**,
A MAILBOX IN THE SHAPE OF A MOLAR AND A TOOTH-FAIRY STATUE
BY THE FRONT DOOR MADE OUT OF **BRICKS**.

A GLANCE AT HIS MOTHER REVEALED
SHE TOO STARED IN AMAZEMENT AND **SHOCK**,
ANXIOUSLY EXITING THE CAR, CURIOUS ABOUT
WHAT OTHER WONDERS THEY'D SEE WHILE VISITING THE **DOC**.

A WALK THROUGH THE DOOR REVEALED
A FLURRY OF MOVEMENT AND FAST-PACED **ACTION**,
CHILDREN SMILING, LAUGHING AND PLAYING WITH
WONDROUS DENTAL **CONTRAPTIONS**.

FLOSS THAT FLOATED THROUGH
THE AIR AND MAGICALLY WORKED ON ITS **OWN**,
A WALKING, TALKING TOOTHBRUSH THAT
GAVE TUTORIALS ON HOW TO STAY A CAVITY FREE **ZONE**.

THE NURSES AND ASSISTANTS WERE DRESSED
IN CLOTHES THE MOST PRISTINE SHADE OF **WHITE**,
AND NOT A SPECK OF DUST OR DIRT WAS
VISIBLE THROUGHOUT THE ENTIRE OFFICE - SUCH A MARVELOUS **SIGHT**!

WITHOUT A WORD BEING UTTERED
OR SOUND BEING **SHARED**,
THE STAFF HURRIED CHARLIE AND HIS MOTHER AWAY,
STILL IN DISBELIEF AT EACH OTHER THEY **STARED**.

A RIDE ON A SHINY SILVER COASTER THROUGH
A HALL WITH PICTURES OF SATISFIED **SMILES**,
THEY WHIZZED THROUGH CORRIDORS AND TUNNELS
THAT ZIGZAGGED FOR WHAT SEEMED LIKE **MILES**.

UNTIL FINALLY THEY SLOWED AND POPPED THROUGH A **DOOR**,
UNLIKE ANY OTHER THEY'D EVER WITNESSED **BEFORE**.

IT WAS SHAPED LIKE A HUMAN MOUTH DOWN TO THE LAST **DETAIL**,
SURELY IT WAS HAND-CRAFTED BECAUSE THIS COULDN'T
BE BOUGHT AT A STORE THAT SOLD TYPICAL **RETAIL**.

A CAREFUL STEP OFF THE RIDE AND BRISKLY WHISKED
INTO THE MYSTERIOUS **ROOM**,

FROM BEHIND A SHIMMERING CURTAIN APPEARED DR. EDWARD NAMMELL
TO APPLAUSE, CONFETTI, AND A THUNDEROUS **BOOM!!**

"GOOD MORNING, SALUTATIONS AND WELCOME,
SO GLAD TO HAVE YOU **HERE**."
"PLEASE TAKE A SEAT IN MY STATE-OF-THE-ART
AND ONE-OF-A-KIND BICUSPID **CHAIR**."

CHARLIE GLEEFULLY HOPPED INTO THE AERODYNAMIC
SPACESHIP LOOKING **POD**,
IT HUGGED HIS BODY WHICH FELT GOOD BUT AT THE SAME TIME
WAS ALSO QUITE **ODD**.

DOC NAMMELL OFFERED A GLANCE, A POKE AND A QUIZZICAL **STARE**,
THEN A BUTTON WAS PUSHED TO SPIN CHARLIE IN THE DOC'S
FUTURISTIC TOOTH **CHAIR**.

FASTER AND FASTER AND FASTER UNTIL THE ROOM WAS A DIZZYING **DAZE**,
THE CHAIR SPUN SO QUICKLY THAT HIS VISION BECAME A BLUR FILLED **HAZE**.

HE HEARD ANOTHER BUTTON GET PUSHED AND ABRUPTLY CAME TO A **STOP**,
TO FIND DOC NAMMELL STANDING THERE WITH A BUCKET AND **MOP**.

"DON'T MIND THESE, ONLY FOR EMERGENCIES YOU SEE,"
HE SAID WITH A **GRIN**.
"WE'RE WELL ON OUR WAY, YOU AND I, NOW THE FUN STUFF **BEGINS**!"

"REJOICE, CHARLIE MY BOY, BECAUSE TODAY YOU'RE IN **LUCK**,"
" I CAN FIX YOUR TEETH NO PROBLEM AND TO DO
IT ALL I'LL NEED IS YOUR **TRUST**."

"YOU MIGHT FIND THIS HARD TO BELIEVE, WHEN I WAS YOUNG
I HAD THE SAME TROUBLES AS **YOU**,"
"AND NOW MY TEETH ARE AS STRAIGHT AS AN ARROW AND YOURS WILL BE **TOO**."

DOC HELD UP A PICTURE OF HIMSELF AS A KID
AND HIS BRACES WERE SHINY AND **BRIGHT**,
CHARLIE CRINGED AT THE THOUGHT OF METAL IN HIS MOUTH
THAT WOULD MAKE HIM LOOK LIKE A HUMAN **FLASHLIGHT**.

"NOT TO BE WORRIED, THE FASHION OF BRACES
HAS CHANGED QUITE A **BIT**,"
"FROM THE COLORS, TO THE MATERIALS,
AND MOST IMPORTANTLY THE **FIT**."

DOC NAMMELL STEPPED ON A SWITCH AND OUT SLID A WALL
WITH BRACES **GALORE**,
"CHARLIE, WHAT WE HAVE HERE IS THE COOLEST REALIGNMENT
AND TOOTH REPAIR **STORE**

"YOUR TEETH SITUATION ISN'T TOO BAD NOR CONSIDERED **SEVERE**,"
"AND BECAUSE OF THAT YOU GET YOUR PICK
OF ANYTHING THAT YOU SEE **HERE**."

"YOU CAN GO WITH INVISIBLE, LINGUAL, CERAMIC OR **METAL**."
"OR PERHAPS YOU WANT FANCY SPINNERS THAT GLOW
RED HOT LIKE A **KETTLE**."

CHARLIE'S MOTHER SMILED WITH JOY BECAUSE FOR THE FIRST TIME
SHE SAW HIM **DELIGHT**,
WITH THE IDEA OF GETTING BRACES, HER HEART WARMED TO THE CORE
TO WITNESS THIS **SIGHT**.

"DOC, THIS IS SUCH GREAT NEWS AND THE BRACES ALL SEEM
REALLY REALLY **COOL**,"
"BUT WHAT ABOUT THE BULLIES, MEAN WORDS AND THINGS
I STILL HAVE TO FACE AT **SCHOOL**?"

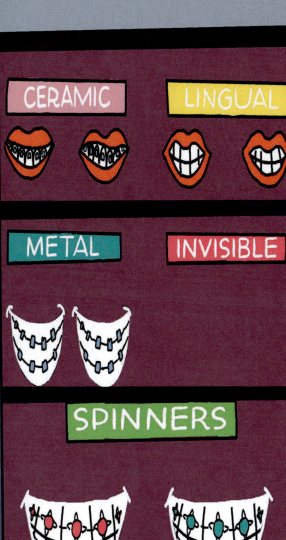

"WELL CHARLIE I DON'T MAKE PROMISES I CAN'T KEEP
SO I'LL GIVE YOU GREAT **NEWS**,"
"IF YOU CAN BE STRONG FOR 2 YEARS, YOUR TEETH WILL BE PERFECT
AND CHANGE ALL OF THEIR **VIEWS**."

"TAKE THIS TO HEART AND ALWAYS KEEP THIS IN **MIND**!"
"IT'S WHAT'S INSIDE OF YOU, NOT STRAIGHT TEETH OR THE MAGIC
OF BRACES THAT GIVE YOU YOUR **SHINE**!"

"YOU ARE GOING THROUGH A PHASE,
LIKE MOST CHILDREN **DO**,"
"BUT WHILE IT MAY SEEM PAINFUL RIGHT NOW,
REST ASSURED THAT YOU'RE GOING TO PULL **THROUGH**."

"NOW PICK OUT THE ONES YOU LIKE BEST MY BOY
AND LET'S GET THESE RIGHT **IN**,"
"BECAUSE THE SOONER WE DO THAT
THEN THE TRANSFORMATION CAN **BEGIN**."

CHARLIE PICKED OUT HIS FAVORITES
AND INTO HIS MOUTH THEY **WENT,**
AND NO MATTER THE COST HIS MOM KNEW
IT WAS MONEY WELL **SPENT.**

FOR AS THEY DROVE AWAY FROM THAT MARVELOUS PLACE
THAT DEFIED SPACE AND **TIME,**
SHE ALREADY FELT THE CHANGE WITHIN HIM AND KNEW
IT WAS CHARLIE'S TIME TO SHINE!

STAY TUNED FOR THE NEXT BOOK IN THE SCHOOLHOUSE SUPER SQUAD SERIES...

Made in the USA
Middletown, DE
17 August 2022